Jackie Robinson was the first Black player
in the major leagues.

Eleven and a half weeks later, on July 5, 1947,
Larry Doby became the second.

ALL STAR

How Larry Doby
Smashed the Color Barrier in Baseball

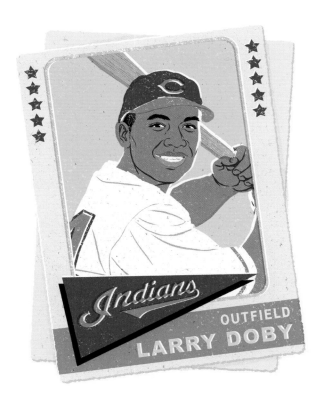

by Audrey Vernick

Illustrated by Cannaday Chapman

Clarion Books | Houghton Mifflin Harcourt | Boston   New York

The boys in Larry Doby's neighborhood—tall and short, Black and white, slow and fast—all played baseball together. Many heard an announcer in their head, giving the play-by-play of every throw and catch.

When young Larry stepped
to the plate, he longed to hear:

Now batting

...atting

...atting

for the Brooklyn Dodgers

...odgers

...odgers

LARRY

...ARRY

...ARRY

DOBY

...OBY

...OBY

But while Larry was growing up in the 1920s and '30s, there were no Black players in Major League Baseball. None. The door was closed to Black players.

It didn't seem like a door to Larry. Doors can open. To him, it looked like a wall. His world didn't even allow him to *dream* of reaching the major leagues.

The world would have to change.

When Larry was a boy in Camden, South Carolina, the South was largely
segregated, but his neighborhood was not. "I went to one school, they went to
another school," Larry said. "And when school was out, we came home. We lived
on the same block and we played . . . and we never thought about color."

Back then everyone listened to sports on the radio. It sometimes felt like the whole country was listening together, especially during boxer Joe Louis's fights. "When he would [win], everyone in the neighborhood would come out and have something like a cheerleading rally because we were all so happy about it."

At age fourteen, Larry moved to New Jersey, where many schools were still segregated, though not the one he attended. He was an all-state athlete in baseball, football, and basketball at Eastside High School in Paterson, and often the only Black player on the team. "I couldn't wait for school to get out, to get on the football field or basketball court or baseball field. I just waited for that bell to ring."

Looking back, there was a historical moment on that high school football field: a meeting of two men who would someday each be famous for being second. In a big game against Montclair High School, Larry scored the winning touchdown. The Montclair team had a player named Buzz Aldrin, who, in 1969, would be the second man to walk on the moon. "Given the circumstances at that time," Larry said, "you could say that I had as much chance then of getting to play in the major leagues as Aldrin did of going to the moon."

The world would have to change.

Larry was such a good ballplayer that while still in high school, he played for the Newark Eagles, a team in the Negro Leagues. The Negro Leagues were baseball leagues specifically for Black and other nonwhite players, providing the only opportunity for them to play professionally. Even so, Larry didn't imagine a future playing baseball. He hoped for a college scholarship and to find a job as a high school coach.

That dream came true. Sort of. He received a scholarship, but was forced to leave school when he was drafted into the Navy. He was stationed at bases around the country before he was sent to Ulithi, an island in the South Pacific.

That's where Larry heard some surprising news.

"It came on the radio that Mr. Branch Rickey had signed Jackie Robinson to play for the [Brooklyn] Dodgers organization." Larry knew Jackie from the Negro Leagues.

Maybe the world was starting to change.

After the war, Larry returned to the Newark Eagles, playing second base. He was starting to think he might have a career in baseball. Larry helped his team win the Negro League World Series in 1946.

That year, Jackie Robinson was playing with the minor league Montreal Royals. The next season, Jackie made his major-league debut with the Dodgers. He was voted Rookie of the Year. But he faced terrible racism. Opposing players and spectators alike screamed insults. There were threats made against him and his family.

The world can be a mess when it's changing.

But it had started to change.

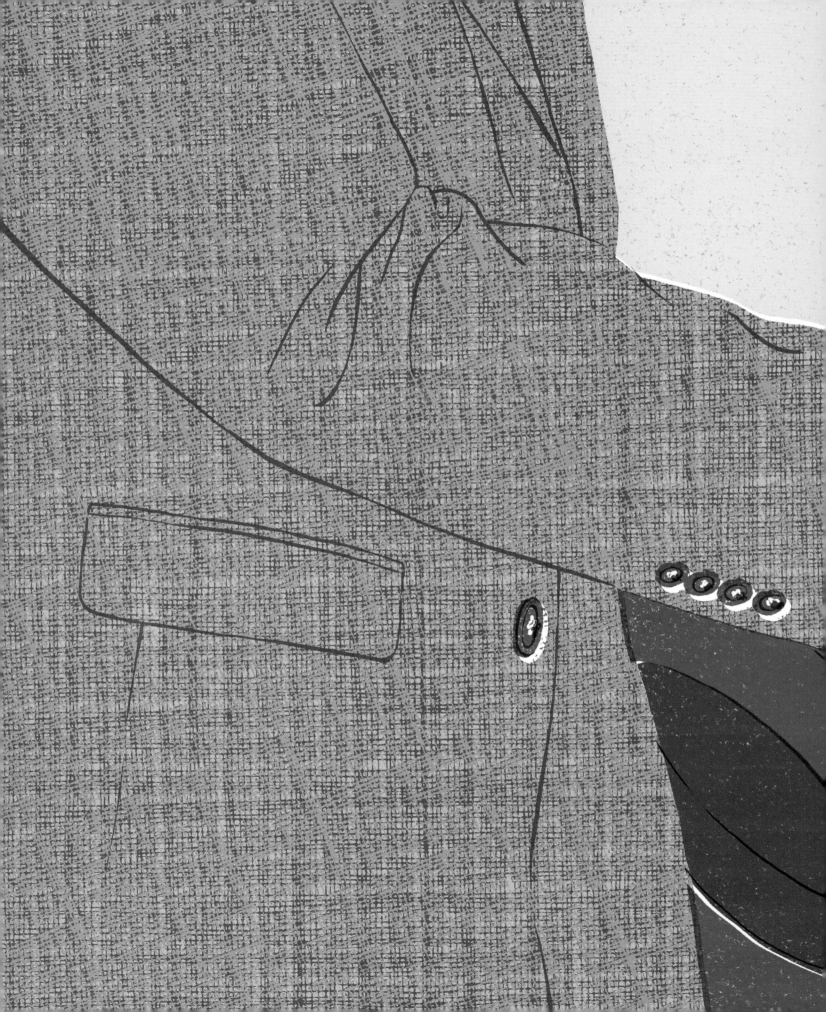

Jackie opened the door. And Larry followed closely behind when team owner Bill Veeck signed him to the Cleveland Indians.

Larry had enormous respect and affection for Veeck. "I was fortunate enough to have a fine man to work for, probably one of the nicest and greatest men I have ever met, because even at that particular time, he never showed any prejudice or bigotry."

Unlike Jackie, Larry didn't play in the minor leagues first.
He went straight from the Negro Leagues to the major leagues.
   "I'd like to say that Jackie made it easy for me," Larry said,
"but I didn't see any difference. Eleven weeks did not alter
the course of race relations in this country."

Larry knew that Jackie Robinson had faced terrible racism and hatefulness from his teammates, opponents, and fans when he joined the Dodgers in the National League. As the first Black player in the American League, Larry did not expect things to be much better. He wasn't wrong. His first day with the Indians was one he always remembered—not in a good way. Some teammates

refused to shake Larry's hand and two turned their backs on him. When he went on the field to warm up, no one would throw the ball with him. "I had never been so alone in my life," he said. "I stood there alone in front of the dugout for five minutes."

But that was just the beginning. He could not stay at white-only hotels with the team and could not enter some stadiums through the main entrance. He often had to eat alone. He was called horrible, unspeakable names, and was spit on by an opposing infielder.

Larry thought of racist people as "sick." He knew there was nothing he could do to heal them.

Baseball Hall of Famer Willie Mays said, "Larry Doby put in just as hard a time as Jackie Robinson. Those two go hand in hand."

In 1948, Larry moved from the infield to the outfield and started playing even better. He helped the Indians win the World Series, the biggest moment of his career. In Game 4, Larry made history when he hit the game-winning home run.

A photograph was taken of Larry celebrating with winning pitcher Steve Gromek.

"When the last out had been made and the game was over, he ran up and we embraced each other," Larry said.

When you look at the picture, you see the kinds of enormous smiles usually found on boys' faces, not men's. Steve's arms are wrapped around Larry's neck. Gromek's mouth is open in the best kind of huge, gleeful grin.

It is a picture of pure joy.

When that picture appeared in newspapers, it really surprised people.

"I think it might have been the first time that a picture like that—a white man embracing a black man—went all over the country. . . . That picture represents one of the finest moments in my life."

And it shows exactly how the world was changing.

Larry Doby was a true star, named to the All-Star team the next year. And the next. And the next, next, next, next, next. Seven years in a row.

The world was changing, but progress was slow. As each player took his turn, he opened doors to those behind him, with more Black players joining the major leagues each year. Barriers take time to fall, and this one took a really long time. It wasn't until 1959 that every baseball team was integrated—the Boston Red Sox were the last to sign a Black player.

But change didn't stop there. Change never stops. Yesterday's players opened the door for today's, and today's players are opening doors for those lined up behind them.

We honor the people who lived through impossibly hard times by continuing their fight on the field and off.

The world doesn't change all by itself. People change the world. People with strength and confidence. It takes a superstar on the field and off.

A man like

LARRY
...ARRY
...ARRY

DOBY
...OBY
...OBY

who achieved way beyond his own boyhood dreams.

AUTHOR'S NOTE

Lawrence Eugene Doby was born on December 13, 1923, in Camden, South Carolina, the son of David and Etta Doby. His father, a talented athlete, died when Larry was eight. Larry's mother moved north to earn money, and Larry spent many of his boyhood years in the care of different relatives before joining his mother in Paterson, New Jersey. He was a gifted athlete like his dad, and that opened many doors. After serving in the Navy, he married his high school sweetheart, Helyn Curvy.

Larry Doby had many impressive baseball achievements, but his story is often overlooked as Jackie Robinson was the first to break the color barrier in Major League Baseball. But Larry had his share of firsts too:

First player for whom a Major League owner negotiated with and paid Negro League owners. (Branch Rickey didn't pay the Kansas City Monarchs when he signed Jackie Robinson.)

First player to go straight from playing in the Negro Leagues to the majors.

First Black ballplayer in the American League.

First Black ballplayer to hit a home run in the World Series.

First Black ballplayer to be on a World Series championship team.

First Black ballplayer to win the RBI title in the American League.

For all his firsts, Larry Doby was destined to forever be second to men named Robinson. First, there was Jackie. And thirty-one years later, Larry was the second Black man to manage a major league team, the Chicago White Sox. Frank Robinson was the first. It is worth celebrating firsts (and seconds), but breaking through the color barrier was just the beginning of a very long process. And progress was far from universal.

Credit: Bettmann/Getty

Steve Gromek and Larry Doby in their famous World Series embrace. Note the racist Cleveland Indians logo on Doby's uniform sleeve, a version of which existed until 2019, when it was finally dropped. In late 2020, the decision was made to also change the team name. As this book went to press, the Cleveland team did not yet have a new moniker. Change continues, but slowly.

When Larry, now a celebrated World Series hero, returned to Paterson, New Jersey, in 1948 to buy a home with Helyn, residents of that all-white neighborhood started a petition to stop them. Ultimately, the mayor of Paterson stepped up to help. Larry and Helyn raised five children together.

In forging through very difficult circumstances, Larry helped clear the road for those behind him. "If you can take the negatives and make them positive, then you're making it better for the next person who comes along," he said.

But to this day, the number of Black major-league ballplayers is notably low. For a variety of reasons, the majority of Black athletes pursue other sports, and representation in the major leagues has been declining. Change is rarely made in an orderly way.

Sometimes it's slow. Sometimes we move backwards. But we have to do what we can to help it along, just as Larry Doby did.

Larry's legacy lives on. His statue stands in front of the Cleveland Indians' ballpark, and the team retired his number (14) in 1994. There are baseball fields named for him in his hometown of Camden, South Carolina, and his teenage home in Paterson, New Jersey.

Larry said that he never played to be remembered. He just wanted to play.

"People and events fade into history," he said. "Even the players today will become dim memories in a future day. The wheel turns."

And the world changes.

SELECTED BIBLIOGRAPHY

Amore, Dom. "Larry Doby Remembers Being Introduced." *Hartford Courant,* April 15, 1997. (articles.courant. com/1997-04-15/sports/9704150685_1_larry-doby-jackie-robinson-modern-major-leagues)

Berkow, Ira. "The Views of a Pioneer." New York Times, August 22, 1985. (www.nytimes.com/1985/08/22/sports/ sports-of-the-times-the-views-of-a-pioneer.html)

Branson, Douglas M. *Greatness in the Shadows: Larry Doby and the Integration of the American League.* Lincoln, NE: University of Nebraska Press, 2016.

Gallagher, Mickey. "Baseball's Larry Doby: #2 but First-Class All the Way Home." *People's World*, April 17, 2018. (www.peoplesworld.org/article/baseballs-larry-doby-2-but-first-class-all-the-way-home)

Izenberg, Jerry. "Larry Doby Should Be Honored by Newark." Star-Ledger, NJ.com, July 7, 2012. (www.nj.com/ sports/ledger/izenbergcol/index.ssf/2012/07/izenberg_larry_doby_should_be.html)

Marshall, William J. "Interview with Lawrence E. Doby, November 15, 1979." Louie B. Nunn Center for Oral History, University of Kentucky Libraries. (kentuckyoralhistory.org/catalog/xt7q5717nx51; accessed 2016)

Moore, Joseph Thomas. *Larry Doby: The Struggle of the American League's First Black Player.* Mineola, NY: Dover Publications, 2011.

Swenson, Kyle. "Larry Doby: Congress Finally Agrees on Race and Equality—When It Comes to a Baseball Legend." *Washington Post*, July 12, 2018. (www.washingtonpost.com/news/morning-mix/wp/2018/07/11/ larry-doby-congress-finally-agrees-on-race-and-equality-when-it-comes-to-a-baseball-legend/?utm_term=. cb1902da0f18)

Wilber, Cynthia J. *For the Love of the Game: Baseball Memories from the Men Who Were There.* New York: William Morrow and Company, Inc., 1992.

For Gbemi . . . emi . . . emi!
—A.V.

To my brother Aaron, who just became a father. His parenting skills
make me prouder and prouder every day. His relationship with his son
was the inspiration for the father and son illustration.
—C.C.

CLARION BOOKS
3 Park Avenue
New York, New York 10016

Text copyright © 2022 by Audrey Vernick
Illustrations copyright © 2022 by Cannaday Chapman

Clarion Books is an imprint of
Houghton Mifflin Harcourt Publishing Company.

hmhbooks.com

The illustrations in this book were done digitally.
The text was set in Adelle.

Library of Congress Cataloging-in-Publication Data is available.
ISBN 978-1-328-48297-6

Manufactured in China
SCP 10 9 8 7 6 5 4 3 2 1
4500831571